ULTIMATE SPORTS

T0120409

TAKE A DEEP BREATH!

EXTREME WATER SPORTS

CHERITON
CHILDREN'S BOOKS

Published in 2024 by **Cheriton Children's Books**
1 Bank Drive West, Shrewsbury, Shropshire, SY3 9DJ, UK

© 2024 Cheriton Children's Books

First Edition

Author: Sarah Eason
Designer: Paul Myerscough
Editor: Jennifer Sanderson
Proofreader: Katie Dicker

Picture credits: Cover: Shutterstock/Wonderful Nature. Inside: p1: Shutterstock/Marc Calleja, pp2-3: Shutterstock/Aastels, p4b: Shutterstock/Wonderful Nature, p4t: Shutterstock/Icemanphotos, p5b: Shutterstock/Wallenrock, p5t: Shutterstock/Ammit Jack, p6: Shutterstock/Dudarev Mikhail, p7: Shutterstock/Dudarev Mikhail, p8: Shutterstock/Dudarev Mikhail, p9: Shutterstock/VicPhotoria, p10: Shutterstock/Jellyman Photography, p11c: Shutterstock/2p2play, p11t: Shutterstock/MemoryMan, pp12-13: Shutterstock/Timophey Akulich, p12b: Shutterstock/Image Source Trading Ltd, p12t: Shutterstock/Kichigin, p13b: Shutterstock/Kitamu, p13t: Shutterstock/AshtonEa, p14: Shutterstock/Creative Cat Studio, p15: Shutterstock/Chameleon Pictures, p16: Shutterstock/Ohrim, p17: Shutterstock/Kaschibo, p17c: Wikimedia Commons/Noah Hamilton, p18: Shutterstock/Sunart Media, p19: Shutterstock/Dudarev Mikhail, p20b: Shutterstock/Maxisport, p20t: Shutterstock/Kovop, p21: Sophie Etheridge, pp22-23: Shutterstock/Marc Calleja, p22b: Wikimedia Commons/Dennis_Daletzki, p22t: Shutterstock/Haripat Jantawalee, p23b: Shutterstock/Victor Maschek, p23c: Shutterstock/Ramon Carretero, p23t: Shutterstock/Sue Robinson, p24: Dreamstime/Sandy Matzen, p25c: Shutterstock/Kuznetcov Konstantin, p25t: Shutterstock/Alesia Puzhauskaite, pp26-27: Shutterstock/Ohrim, p26b: Shutterstock/Alesia Puzhauskaite, p26t: Shutterstock/Chiyacat, p27b: Shutterstock/Vojko Berk, p27t: Shutterstock/Nubbin, p28: Shutterstock/Wallenrock, p29b: Shutterstock/Anna Moskvina, p29c: Wikimedia Commons/Robbynaishus1111, p30: Shutterstock/Yuriy_fx, p31: Shutterstock/Martin Charles Hatch, p32b: Shutterstock/Alvov, p32t: Shutterstock/Darren Baker, p33b: Wikimedia Commons/Laura Dekker, pp34-35: Shutterstock/Artur Didyk, p35b: Shutterstock/Ammit Jack, pp36-37: Shutterstock/Artur Didyk, p36b: Shutterstock/VE Studio, p36c: Wikimedia Commons/Martijn Munneke, p37b: Shutterstock/Dmitry Pichugin, p37t: Shutterstock/Howard Sandler, p38: Shutterstock/DawidAndMarcelina, p39: Shutterstock/EpicStockMedia, p40b: Shutterstock/EpicStockMedia, p40t: Shutterstock/Flystock, p41b: Wikimedia Commons/Madeleine Ball, pp42-43: Shutterstock/Georgios Tsichlis, p42b: Shutterstock/HandmadePictures, p42c: Shutterstock/Monicami, p43b: AdobeStock/David Chantre, p43c: Shutterstock/Cegli, p43t: Shutterstock/W Verhagen, pp44-45: Shutterstock/Aastels, p46b: Shutterstock/Artur Didyk, p46t: Shutterstock/Maksym Fesenko, p47t: Shutterstock/EpicStockMedia.

Printed in China

Please visit our website,
www.cheritonchildrensbooks.com
to see more of our high-quality books.

CONTENTS

TAKE A DEEP BREATH!

Much of our planet is covered in water—that's why it's known as the Blue Planet. When seen from space, our blue world looks magical, and it is. The beauty and power of the world's lakes, rivers, seas, and oceans **captivate** the most **extreme sportspeople** on Earth, who use our watery wonderworld as a thrill-seeker's playground.

THE EXTREME DREAM

For centuries, people have played in the oceans—swimming in them, diving in them, surfing on them, and sailing across them. Today, some extreme **athletes** have taken these activities to a whole new level, diving deeper than ever before, riding ever-bigger waves, and sailing farther than they thought possible. Experiencing the ultimate sport has become the ultimate dream.

READY TO EXPLORE THE EXTREME? THEN, TAKE A DEEP BREATH AND DIVE IN!

CHAPTER 1

THE ULTIMATE DIVERS

Beneath the ocean's surface is a world unlike any other—it is a world that is utterly magical, and utterly silent. This underwater paradise draws in divers, who sink into its depths to discover a wealth of nature.

FREE TO DIVE

Most divers explore the watery wonderland with a lot of diving equipment. But one extreme group of divers plunge into the depths with only a mask, a **wetsuit**, a pair of flippers—and a deep love of the ocean. They are freedivers.

BREATHE DEEP, DIVE DEEP

Freedivers are extraordinary athletes. At the water's surface, they take a deep breath then dive beneath the surface of the ocean, plunging as far as they can. The world's **elite** freedivers can hold their breath underwater for an incredible 10 minutes!

Some freedivers can reach depths of more than 500 feet (152 m) below the surface.

"FREEDIVING— IT'S A RUSH UNLIKE ANY OTHER."

TOTAL CONTROL

Freedivers have trained their bodies to cope with the extreme **pressures** of diving with no equipment. They have learned to slow their **heart rates** so that their bodies use less **oxygen**, and this allows them to remain underwater for longer.

Freedivers also practice resisting the natural urge to breathe while **submerged**, and this control allows them to dive to extraordinary depths on just a single breath.

DIVING TO SURVIVE

Archeologists believe that the ancient people of Chile were freedivers. However, these extreme ancient divers were not diving for fun. Instead, they plunged into the depths to hunt for food and prizes such as pearls and sponges, which they **traded**.

EXTREME HISTORY

Freediving is not a modern sport. Archeologists have found **evidence** that people have been diving beneath the waves for around 8,000 years!

While they were investigating **mummified** remains in a coastal part of Chile, archeologists discovered that people who lived in the area in around 6,000 BCE suffered from exostosis. This is a condition in which the bones of the ear canal begin to grow across the opening of the ear, to protect the **eardrum** from **exposure** to cold water.

Many people who practice water sports, from surfers and **kayakers** to windsurfers and divers, have exostosis.

A RISK WORTH TAKING

Freediving comes with risks. There is a danger that divers can become **disoriented** underwater. Their eardrums may burst because of the extreme pressure their ears experience. There is also the risk that divers will **lose consciousness** beneath the waves and never make it back to the surface. So, why do it?

FINDING FREEDOM

Many freedivers talk of a feeling of supreme freedom when they dive and of being deeply connected with nature. Some say that the silence underwater allows them to connect fully with the visual beauty around them, and this **exhilarating** freediving experience makes the danger of diving a risk worth taking.

EXTREME STARS

FREEDIVING FAMILY

One of the greatest freedivers in the world today is Alexey Molchanov. Born in 1987, the Russian diver holds numerous records. He also comes from a family of great divers: His mother Natalia was one of the world's best female freedivers.

A WATER BABY

Natalia loved swimming and being in the water, and so she inspired her son to love water sports too. By the time he was five years old, Alexey was showing signs of being a great swimmer, and he soon began to win races and break records. Then, in 2002, Natalia discovered freediving, and introduced her son to it too.

The beauty of the natural world beneath the waves is a draw for many freedivers.

These freedivers are swimming in extremely cold water off the coast of Iceland. On the day of Alexey's dive in Lake Baikal, in 2021, the water was a freezing 37 degrees Fahrenheit (3 °C)!

ALEXEY DESCRIBES FREEDIVING AS A UNIQUE EXPERIENCE THAT MAKES YOU REALIZE HOW SMALL YOU ARE IN THE ENORMITY OF THE OCEAN— AND THE ENTIRE UNIVERSE.

RECORD BREAKING AND TRAGEDY

In 2004, Alexey entered and won his first freediving competition, diving to 518 feet (158 m) in a swimming pool. Over the next 10 years, he went on to break a series of records, alongside his mother. Then, in 2015 when Natalia was teaching a freediving lesson off the coast of Formentera, near Ibiza in the Mediterranean Sea, **tragedy** struck. Natalia dove beneath the waves but she never resurfaced. Natalia's body was never found, and she was believed likely dead. Alexey was distraught and felt that if only he had been with his mother during the dive, the accident would never have happened.

A WORLD OF WINS

Despite his loss, Alexey did not give up freediving. He returned to the ocean to explore its depths again and went on to win a string of medals and to break countless records. In 2021, Alexey even braved freezing water to set another record by diving 262 feet (80 m) below the surface of Lake Baikal in Siberia, Russia. Today, he holds more than 25 world records and has won the World Championships in freediving a staggering number of times.

CAVE DIVING

One of the most extreme of all sports has to be cave exploration—and even more so when it is done underwater! Cave diving is especially dangerous because it involves traveling through caves that have often not yet been **navigated**. These caves can be full of dangers too, including falling rocks that can trap a diver in narrow, winding tunnels. The tunnels can be dark, disorienting, and deadly.

TRAINING FOR DANGER

Cave divers need to use high-tech equipment to carry out their sport. They dive with **oxygen tanks**, masks, wetsuits, and flippers. Becoming a qualified cave diver can take many years of training because the sport is so difficult and dangerous.

EXTREME
NEED TO KNOW

Cave diving should not be confused with cavern diving —the two are quite different. Cavern diving involves diving in an open area that gets sunlight and has a depth of no more than 70 feet (21 m). This type of diving also takes place within 130 feet (40 m) of a cave entrance.

Cave diving involves exploration often many miles underwater and in areas that do not have natural light. **Visibility** is often reduced, which is another reason why cave diving can be so difficult and dangerous.

Cave diving requires so much training and is so highly skilled that just 1 percent of the world's divers are cave divers!

An example of a wet and dry **cave network** is the Tham Luang cave system in Thailand, in which a Thai youth soccer team became stranded in 2018. A team of highly experienced cave divers rescued the players and their coach, and their story made headlines around the world.

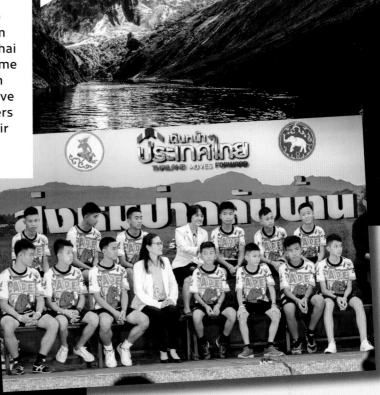

"CAVE DIVING—IT'S MY PASSION."

SPRING OR SUMP?

Cave divers define cave dives as either spring or sump dives. Spring dives take place in water that is usually clear and flowing. In this type of water, divers move with the flow of the water while holding a **guideline**.

Sump diving takes place in both wet and dry cave networks. They are usually murky and dark, and can be made up of a mixture of underwater caves and dry caves.

DIVES

For elite cave divers, Earth's underground caves and caverns are a mysterious and magical draw. These are some of the top sites on their bucket list.

Cenote Angelita

Where: Mexico

The draw: a mix of **fresh water** and **salt water**, with a maximum depth of 200 feet (61 m)

Ben's Cave

Where: Grand Bahama, the Caribbean

The draw: one of the longest freshwater cave systems, and full of amazing features such as **stalactites**, **stalagmites**, and **fossilized** shells

Indian Springs

Where: Florida, United States

The draw: believed to be the best cave dive in North America

Nereo Cave

Where: Sardinia, Italy

The draw: the largest underwater cave in the Mediterranean Sea, it has spectacular arches and tunnels

Emergence du Ressel

Where: France

The draw: has a 2.5-mile- (4 km) long loop that divers try to complete, but few do

Kilsby Sinkhole

Where: Australia

The draw: a 213-feet- (65 m) deep cave filled with beautiful crystal-clear water

Orda Cave

Where: Russia

The draw: the longest cave in Russia with many tiny passages that challenge even the most experienced of divers

Anhumas Abyss

Where: Brazil

The draw: an amazing underground lake filled with huge **schools** of fish

Chinhoyi Caves

Where: Zimbabwe

The draw: divers love the network of interesting tunnels and caves, filled with amazingly clear water

CHAPTER 2

SURFACE THRILL-SEEKERS

Break through the water's surface and take a deep breath, because it's here that some of the most extreme **adrenaline**-powered sports on Earth take place! The deep may draw in extreme sportspeople who are willing to risk all for the thrill they experience in the water, but so too does the ocean's surface. From windsurfing and wakeboarding to open water swimming and surfing, the water's surface is a playground for ultimate sports lovers.

This surfer is using a shortboard, which is good for tricks because it's easy to **maneuver** and can make quick turns.

"SURFING ISN'T JUST A SPORT—IT'S A WAY OF LIFE."

WAVE RIDERS

Have you ever watched a surfer catch a wave then ride it as it curls over their head, while they twist and turn beneath the **crest**? It is amazing to see, and for the surfer, it's one of the most exhilarating rides on Earth.

SURFING—THE LONG AND THE SHORT

For a surfer, their board is everything. But most surfers have a preferred type—longboard or shortboard. Longboards came first. They were used in the early days of surfing and were made from wood, so they were really heavy—on average, they weighed 100 pounds (45 kg). And like their name suggests, they were long, reaching up to 20 feet (6 m) in length.

LIGHTENING UP

Today, longboards measure up to 10 feet (3 m) long. Most modern longboards weigh around 15 pounds (6.8 kg), which is light compared to the weighty original boards. In the early days of surfing, carrying a heavyweight longboard to the water must have been an extreme sport in its own right.

EXTREME HISTORY

We know that surfing dates all the way back to 3,000 years ago, when surfers in Hawaii and the **Polynesian Islands** rode wooden longboards across the waves for fun.

SHORTER AND EASIER

Faster across the water's surface and easier to ride are shortboards. The boards are up to just 6.5 feet (2 m) long, and are also lighter than longboards, weighing around 5 pounds (2.3 kg) on average.

Longboards are more stable. They have a greater surface area in the water and more room for your feet, which helps with balance.

It takes an amazing amount of balance and skill to ride a board across the ocean's surface, and the greatest surfers in the world take on waves that are up to 70 feet (21 m) tall.

WAVE HUNTERS

For serious surfers, riding the world's biggest and most challenging waves is their goal. And many shape their lives around this **pursuit**, traveling all over the world to find the best waves.

STUNT SURFERS

Extreme surfers have made wave riding an art form, performing incredible moves on their boards. Stunts that some of the world's most skilled surfers show off include flips and leaps in the air and quick changes in the direction of the board.

EXTREME NEED TO KNOW

Like all extreme sports, surfing comes with dangers. Surfers can be caught in **undertows** when they come off their boards, and can drown. They are also at risk of being tossed against rocks, and occasional shark attacks have been known to take place.

SHARKS AND SURFERS

Although they are rare, encounters between surfers and sharks do happen. There have been a number of documented events, including one in 2023, when **professional** surfer Max Marsden was enjoying some early-morning surfing off the west coast of Australia.

FIGHTING BACK

As Max surfed, a bronze whaler shark attacked and bit into his arm. Amazingly, Max managed to fight off the shark and make it back to the shore. He was taken to a hospital for immediate surgery, and lived to tell his story.

TIGER THREAT

Probably the most famous surfer victim of a shark attack is Bethany Hamilton from Hawaii. A tiger shark attacked Bethany while she was surfing in 2003. She was just 13 years old and lost her left arm to the shark, but was lucky to survive the attack.

SURVIVING AND SURFING

After the attack, it seemed that Bethany's surfing future hung in the balance, but with complete determination, she quickly returned to the ocean. With a **custom-made** board, Bethany learned to surf one-armed, and amazingly returned to the sport less than a month after the shark attack took place. She has since gone on to become one of the world's most successful female surfers.

Although she lost an arm in the **traumatic** shark attack, Bethany hasn't lost her love of surfing.

DESPITE HER AMAZING ACHIEVEMENTS, BETHANY IS **MODEST**, DESCRIBING HERSELF AS "JUST A SURFER!"

OUT IN THE OPEN

Open water swimming is described as swimming in outdoor areas of water such as rivers, lakes, and oceans. Outdoor bodies of water are often cold, so many people choose to swim in a wetsuit to keep warm. But some people love the feeling of the cold water against their skin, and brave the waters in a swimsuit.

FEELING FREE

Many people who open water swim say the sport gives them an amazing sense of freedom, with nothing about them but an **expanse** of water and breathtaking natural views. A lot of people also feel a sense of euphoria, or great happiness, when they swim in open water. This is because the body releases a "happy **hormone**" called dopamine when exposed to extreme cold. The hormone makes swimmers feel **elated** during and after their swim.

EXTREME HISTORY

The English **Channel** lies between the United Kingdom (UK) and mainland Europe. It has been the site of many of the earliest long-distance open water swims in recorded history. In 1875, Captain Matthew Webb became the first person to swim across the English Channel, and in 1926, Gertrude Ederle swam the Channel, at just 19 years old.

Goggles are usually worn for open water swimming, and a **swimming buoy** can be used for safety.

"SWIMMING IN OPEN WATER—IT'S A FEELING OF ABSOLUTE FREEDOM."

Many countries famous for winter swimming are found in northern Europe, such as the **Scandinavian countries**, and Eastern Europe, including Ukraine and Russia.

BIG-FREEZE CHALLENGE

Some extreme open water swimmers also take the plunge in incredibly cold winter waters. At the most extreme level, winter swimmers tackle bodies of water so cold, their surfaces have frozen over! Sections of the ice are cut away to allow swimmers to plunge into the ultra-cold water beneath. In competitions, swimmers brave water that can be below 41 degrees Fahrenheit (5 °C).

GOING THE DISTANCE

Open water swimming can be across just short distances, simply for a love of the sport, but more extreme swimmers take the challenge to another level. They swim across incredibly long distances and in very tough waters in **endurance** swimming challenges.

ULTRA SWIMS

Marathon swimming is ultra-long distance swimming across at least 6.2 miles (10 km) of water. In marathon swimming challenges, extreme open water swimmers cover incredible distances.

FAMOUS FOR BEING TOUGH

Some of the most famous and toughest of long-distance swims include swimming the English Channel, the Fehmarn Belt, and the Cook **Strait**. Another famous marathon swimming event is the Triple Crown of Open Water Swimming, which includes three swims: the English Channel, between Catalina Island and mainland southern California, and around Manhattan Island in New York City.

"OPEN WATER SWIMMING DOES NOT HAVE LINES. IT DOES NOT HAVE LANES. IT HAS NO LIMITS."

Long-distance open water swimming is one of the most extreme endurance sports on Earth.

Triathletes train in open water for triathlons, which include open water swimming.

ENDURANCE STAR

Open Water Marathon Swimmer Sophie Etheridge was a student at university who loved swimming, cycling, and running until a cycling accident in 2011. It left her with the conditions Complex Regional Pain Syndrome and Fibromyalgia, which both cause long-term **chronic** pain. Almost overnight, Sophie went from an athlete to a wheelchair user.

RECOVERY

After years of hospital treatments and medications Sophie became **depressed**. She struggled to deal with what had happened to her and with the constant pain she experienced. To help her manage her condition she was sent on a pain management programme, part of which was **therapy** in the water called hydrotherapy. Despite experiencing severe discomfort when in the water she battled through the pain and began swimming again—and loved it!

TOUGH GIRL TRIUMPHS

Swimming turned Sophie's life around. She is now an open water marathon swimmer and is training to swim the English Channel. She is also a swimming teacher, and has created a community of open water swimmers with disabilities working tirelessly to improve access to open water swimming for those with disabilities.

Sophie writes for *The Outdoor Swimmer Magazine*, in which she raises awareness and talks about open water swimming with a disability.

SOPHIE SAYS SHE WAS TERRIFIED TO GET BACK INTO THE WATER AGAIN AFTER HER ACCIDENT, BUT WHEN SHE DID, DESPITE THE DISCOMFORT, SHE FELT A SENSE OF PEACE.

THE WORLD'S GREATEST SWIMS

For elite open water swimmers, Earth's oceans and seas have a wealth of challenges. But of them all, the Oceans Seven is considered the greatest. It is an ultra-marathon swim that includes swimming across seven of the world's deadliest channels.

The North Channel

Where: between Ireland and Scotland

The dangers: rough waters, strong **currents**, and jellyfish

The Tsugaru Strait

Where: between the islands of Honshu and Hokkaido, Japan

The dangers: rough waters, large waves, and jellyfish

The Molokai Channel

Where: between Oahu and Molokai Islands, Hawaii

The dangers: strong currents, deep water, and deadly jellyfish

The Catalina Channel

Where: between Santa Catalina Island and southern California

The dangers: great white sharks

The English Channel

Where: between the southern UK and France

The dangers: cold waters, jellyfish, and passing ships

The Cook Strait

Where: between the North and South Islands of New Zealand

The dangers: cold water, jellyfish, and sharks

The Strait of Gibraltar

Where: between Spain and North Africa

The dangers: sharks, changeable waters, jellyfish, and passing ships

CATCHING THE WIND

Like surfers, windsurfers use nature's power to pull them across the water. Windsurfing is an awesome extreme sport in which people catch the wind in a sail attached to a board to power them incredibly quickly across the water's surface.

SURF STAR

Sarah-Quita Offringa began windsurfing when she was just nine years old. The Dutch sport-loving girl was born in Aruba, an island in the Caribbean Sea, in 1991. She grew up there, where she did almost every type of sport, from dance to karate. Sarah says that her parents made her and her brother Quincy do a lot of sports to keep them from watching TV all day!

DIGGING DEEP, RISING HIGH

Sarah got into windsurfing when Quincy began the sport. She found it difficult at first, and struggled to carry the heavy equipment into the water. But she dug in and did not give up, and it paid off. Sarah practiced and practiced her sport, and in 2018 she won the Professional Windsurfers Association (PWA) World Championship. Then did it again the following year!

To date, Sarah has won the World Championship in windsurfing a staggering 20 times and is considered one of the world's best-ever female windsurfers.

"MY FAVORITE DAYS ARE ACTIVE DAYS—GOING TO THE GYM, HITTING THE WAVES FOR A WINDSURFING SESSION IN THE MORNING, FOLLOWED BY ANOTHER IN THE AFTERNOON!"

The greatest windsurfers can reach incredible speeds on the water and perform amazing stunts.

Flyboarders can shoot up into the air to staggering heights of 45 feet (14 m)!

EXTREME
NEED TO KNOW

Competitive windsurfers take part in three types of competition: freestyle windsurfing, racing, and slalom. Amazing stunts and tricks are performed in freestyle competitions. In racing, top speeds are reached on the water, as they are in slalom, but slalom windsurfers also have to navigate obstacles on the water's surface.

FLYING ACROSS WATER

Like windsurfers, flyboarders are often seen performing tricks above the water's surface. But unlike windsurfers, flyboarders are not powered by sails and the wind. Instead, they wear boots with hoses connected to a jet ski on a board. They use the jet-ski power to **propel** themselves into the air, where they can perform incredible twists, flips, and turns. The jet-ski power can also be used to dive beneath the waves.

THE WORLD'S BEST WINDSURFING ZONES

Windsurfing is all about wind and surf!
For elite windsurfers, these are the best
places in the world to find both.

Bonaire

Where: the Caribbean Sea

The draw: beautiful beaches
and regular winds

Jericoacoara

Where: Brazil

The draw: strong winds and
flat water

Cabarete

Where: the Dominican
Republic

The draw: perfect white sands
and crystal-clear water with
amazing waves

Dakhla

Where: Morocco

The draw: smooth, flat water and strong winds

Maui

Where: Hawaii

The draw: beautiful water and white beaches

Alacati

Where: Turkey

The draw: flat water, beautiful views, and high winds

Vasiliki

Where: Greece

The draw: regular winds and beautiful water

Lake Garda

Where: Italy

The draw: reliable winds and beautiful views

Mauritius

Where: the Indian Ocean

The draw: a mix of calm water and amazing waves, along with high winds and beautiful views

Fuerteventura

Where: the Canary Islands

The draw: the island's name means "strong wind," and it lives up to it with high winds and awesome waves

"THE SUN, THE WIND, AND THE SEA—IT'S ALL YOU NEED TO HAVE A GREAT DAY."

Some kitesurfers can perform incredible leaps into the air.

SPEED, SKY, AND STUNTS

Like windsurfers, kitesurfers use the wind's power to race across the surface of the water, but they do this by capturing the wind in a strong kite rather than a sail. The kite is attached to a strap-on harness that is worn by the kitesurfer, who balances on a single board.

WORLDWIDE WATER LOVERS

Waterskiing is another extreme water sport that is loved around the world. Waterskiers race across the water on two skis as they hold onto a rope that is attached to a boat.

Waterskiers can move at top speeds of 100 miles per hour (160 kph). In competitions, they wow crowds as they perform amazing tricks, including jumps and spins in the air, or they ski around obstacles in slalom competitions while moving at impressive speeds.

BIG BOARDING

Like waterskiing, wakeboarding involves being pulled along the surface of the water by a boat, but on just one board rather than two skis. A wakeboarder holds onto a rope, which is attached to the boat, while balancing on a single board on the water's surface.

HAWAIIAN HERO

Ask any wind or kitesurfer who their greatest all-time hero is, and they'll likely answer "Robby Naish." Robby was born in California in 1963, but his father, who was a surfer, moved the family to Hawaii a few years later, and that is where Robby has since lived. On moving to Hawaii, he soon became a master of the wind and waves.

SLAM DUNK!

Robby started windsurfing when he was just 11 years old, and at 13 years of age, he won his first windsurfing World Championship. He then went on to win championship after championship in the following years, claiming a grand total of 24 world windsurfing titles!

SPORT STAR TO BUSINESSMAN

With one water sport truly under his belt, Robby looked for another—and found kitesurfing. He soon began to master it, along with Stand Up Paddle Boarding (SUP). In 1996, the sports star turned his attention to business and set up Naish Sails Hawaii. His business builds and sells all types of water sport equipment.

ALL-TIME GREAT

Robby is credited with being the first windsurfer to ride giant waves and wave tubes, which usually only surfers are seen to do.

Today, Robby is considered a living sports **legend** and a water sport superstar.

Like waterskiiers, wakeboarders can also perform amazing stunts, leaping into the air to show off jumps and spins.

CHAPTER 3

EXTREME MACHINES

For centuries, people have used machines to travel across the world's lakes, rivers, seas, and oceans. From sailboats to canoes and kayaks, machines have made it possible for us to journey quickly and easily across water. But what was once a need has since become a sport, and today, people use mighty water machines just for (very extreme) fun.

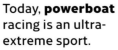

Today, **powerboat** racing is an ultra-extreme sport.

ULTIMATE POWER

For many people, powerboats are the ultimate fun on water. These super-expensive, sleek boats are often seen as the playthings of the rich and famous, and can reach incredible speeds.

RACES AND PLACES

Races can take place both **offshore** and on **inland** waters. Offshore powerboat racing is incredibly popular in the United States, Europe, and Australia. The most powerful boats can reach amazing speeds of up to 160 miles per hour (257 kph). Inland powerboat racing takes place in bays and on lakes and rivers.

MUST-HAVE MACHINE

Like powerboats, jet skis have also become a must-have water machine in vacation areas, and jet skiing is an amazingly popular extreme sport. If you go on a beach vacation, you'll likely see jet skiers shooting across the water's surface and leaping over the waves.

Like all extreme sports, jet ski racing can be dangerous. For that reason, racers often wear helmets, body suits, and other protective coverings to try and prevent injuries if accidents happen.

TO THE NEXT LEVEL

Some extreme jet skiers take the sport to another level by entering competitions. Jet ski racing is especially popular in Australia and the United States. Competitions mainly take place on big lakes, with an oval-shaped course made from buoys. Racers complete a set number of laps around the course, and the first person to complete the laps is the winner.

OCEAN EXPLORERS

Unlike powerboats and jet skis, sailboats have an ancient history. For thousands of years, people have sailed across the world's water in sailboats, capturing the power of the wind in sails and using it to drive them forward. They sailed to travel from place to place, exploring new countries and **trading** goods. But just over 300 years ago, people decided to start sailing for fun, and over time, it became a popular sport.

FOR AMERICA

In 1851, some members of the New York Yacht Club named a newly built **yacht** *America*. It was then sailed to England in the UK, where it went around the Isle of Wight and won a **trophy** called the Hundred Guinea Cup. The world of international yacht racing, and the age of extreme sailing, had begun.

TOUGHEST OF THE TOUGH

Of all the world's toughest sailing events, the most difficult of all is known to be the Golden Globe. In fact, this sailing competition is recognized as probably the toughest human sporting challenge on Earth. The race involves sailing around the world nonstop—and solo, or alone.

Sailboat racing is a tough sport that requires a lot of training and a ton of upper body strength.

Sailing competitions are often fast and furious, with boats traveling incredibly close to one another.

SAILING AND SURVIVING

When the Golden Globe first took place in 1968, no one knew at the time if anyone could sail 30,000 miles (48,000 km) across the seas in one go, and survive. Nine sailors from around the world entered the race, but only one, England's Robin Knox-Johnston, completed it.

AN EXTREME WAIT

It would be another 50 years before the extreme event took place again, in 2018! This time, 18 sailors from 13 different countries took part, with 5 completing the race. Jean-Luc Van Den Heede won the race, navigating the globe in a total of 212 days.
In 2022, the race began once more and history was made when South African Kirsten Neuschäfer became the first woman to win the race.

EXTREME STARS

YOUNG, GIFTED, AND SAILING

In recent years, the world has been gripped by stories of fearless young sailors who have navigated the world's most dangerous seas. In June 2009, at 17 years and 7 months old, Zac Sunderland from California sailed around the world alone, to become the first person under 18 to do so. Six weeks later, he lost his record to British sailor Mike Perham, who circled the globe aged 17 years and 5 months.

NETHERLANDS NEWCOMER

Later in 2009, another sailor came forward to throw her hat in the ring. Laura Dekker from the Netherlands announced that she would sail alone around the world—at just 14 years old!

SOLO SUPERSTAR

When people heard Laura's declaration, many thought it was crazy. The Dutch government tried to stop her, and a court even ordered that she must not make the trip because she was so young. But Laura did not give up, and fought for her right to sail. In 2012, she won, and sailed around the world, alone, aged 16. It was an incredible achievement.

Today, Laura encourages other young sailors to realize their dreams too and take on the world and its amazing oceans.

LAURA SAYS THAT FOR HER, SAILING THE GLOBE WAS NOT ABOUT BREAKING A RECORD, BUT ABOUT DOING SOMETHING THAT SHE REALLY LOVES—SAILING.

NAIL-BITING RIDES

All boating requires a love of being on the water—and a lot of upper body strength, and none more so than kayaking and **whitewater** rafting. These two extreme water sports need a lot of muscle power, and a lot of nerve!

EXTREME EQUIPMENT

A kayak usually holds one person. The boat sits low in the water, with the kayaker in the middle, using a **double paddle** to power the boat forward and steer.

A kayaker wears safety gear, such as a helmet and a personal flotation device, to protect their head and keep them floating in the water if an accident happens.

NOT SO SAFE

Like any body of water, a river also has its dangers, from whirlpools to rapids, which are areas in which the water swirls violently, creating churning whitewater. Ordinary boats could be easily sunk or crushed against the rocks in such conditions. Kayaks were born from a need to create more **streamlined** and **buoyant** boats that could more easily and safely navigate **treacherous** waters.

EXTREME HISTORY

People first started kayaking as a means to get from one place to another. Moving along rivers by boat was often quicker than across land, and sometimes safer in times when wild animals, and people too, were a threat on land.

DEATHLY DROPS

Extreme kayakers love the challenge of rough water, and whitewater kayaking is a draw for many who love the sport. So too are waterfalls, down which extreme kayakers can launch themselves up to 100 feet (30 m) in a white-knuckle drop.

WHIRLING AND WHITE

Whitewater rafts are **inflatable** boats in which a group of people can sit, holding an oar to paddle the boat through the water. Like extreme kayaking, whitewater rafting takes place in rapids.

WATER WORLD

Whitewater rafting is now a fully-fledged sport. Competitions take place in which people navigate a course of gates down rapids as quickly as they can. Many places around the world also offer whitewater rafting trips in which people can try their hand at the sport in beautiful settings such as in New Zealand, Africa, Europe, and parts of North and South America.

Whitewater rafting is a white-knuckle ride!

THE WORLD'S BEST WHITEWATER

Elite kayakers look for extreme challenges when it comes to picking Earth's most awesome kayak zones. Think giant waterfalls, deadly rapids, and a lot of whitewater! Here are the top places in the world to find them.

Zambezi River

Where: Zimbabwe / Zambia

The rush: some of the best whitewater on Earth make this African river a mecca for rafting

Royal Gorge

Where: Colorado, United States

The rush: beautiful waterfalls and big rapids

Tlapacoyan

Where: Mexico

The rush: endless steep waterfalls, awesome freefall sections, and incredible rain forest scenery

Ottawa River

Where: Canada

The rush: a beautiful river with many different types of water make for world-class kayaking

Rondu Gorge

Where: Pakistan

The rush: awesome whitewater and fast-moving flows

White Nile River

Where: Uganda

The rush: massive amounts of whitewater and huge waves

CHAPTER 4

ON A CLIFF EDGE

Extreme sports take place below the water and at its surface, but for some extreme sportspeople, ultimate water adventures begin at the cliff edge.

EXTREME EXPLORERS

Coasteering is one of the most popular extreme sports today. Coasteerers explore both the rocky shores and waters around coastal areas, venturing into caves, jumping off cliffs, and swimming in wild waters. Coasteerers usually wear a wetsuit and a helmet to protect their head from any knocks or falling rocks. They usually dive in groups too, for safety in numbers.

Coasteering is an adrenaline-fueled experience, and people who do it say the rewards make the risky sport worth it.

"YOU HAVE TO TRUST YOURSELF, AND BELIEVE YOU CAN DO IT."

Divers must check what is below the surface of the water before attempting a dive. Underwater rocks are extremely dangerous.

DIG IN AND DIVE!

Imagine standing on the very edge of a cliff, looking down at the water's surface many feet below, and then jumping off. That's cliff diving. It's the ultimate sport for some thrillseekers, and one that is practiced all over the world.

DANGEROUS DIVING

Cliff diving looks dangerous—and it is! Divers train and train to perform their moves as carefully and safely as they can. Since they are diving from incredible heights in many cases, divers need to be sure that they enter the water from the correct angle. If not, they can severely injure themselves.

EXTREME HISTORY

The oldest recorded cliff dive dates back to 1770. Then, King Kahekili II of Maui, Hawaii, carried out a practice known as "lele kawa," which means jumping feet first from a high point without making a splash. The king even insisted that his warriors carry out the practice to show that they had courage and were loyal to him. Later, the practice turned into a competition in which participants were judged on their dives.

BRUTAL TO BODIES

Cliff diving puts an incredible toll on the body. As they hurtle through the air toward the water, divers reach speeds of up to 52 miles per hour (84 kph). Then, they hit the water—hard. On reaching the water's surface, divers smack into it with a force that can be two or three times that of **gravity**. They plunge with such force that they create what is called a "bombhole," which looks like an explosion in the water.

THE BEST DIVERS

Today, cliff diving competitions take place around the world, in some spectacular landscapes. The most famous of them is the Red Bull Cliff Diving World Series, which first took place in 2009. Every year, cliff divers compete to perform the most spectacular dives from platforms 85 to 92 feet (26 to 28 m) above the water's surface.

Cliff diving takes a lot of nerve, and a lot of training.

Cliff diving is becoming more and more popular in sunny coastal places around the world.

On the way down, divers must make sure that their bodies are fully **aligned** so that they enter the water's surface cleanly—anything sticking out is "going to hurt," as one diver said. That is why divers train incredibly hard to keep all their muscles fully **rigid** as they dive, so they make a clean entry into the water.

EXTREME STAR

POOL TO CLIFF TOP

Colombian Orlando Duque was always sporty as a child. He started off playing soccer, then gave pool diving a try. But the brilliant diver soon became bored of leaping off the diving board into a pool, and turned his attention upward—to the cliff tops!

A NATURAL

Orlando is a cliff diving natural and has won an amazing 13 world titles, including nine Red Bull Cliff Diving World Series events. He even appeared in a movie titled *9 Dives*, in which he made the biggest jump of his life—a 111-feet (34 m) dive off a bridge in Italy.

Nicknamed "The Duke," Orlando is considered one of the greatest cliff divers of all time.

ORLANDO DESCRIBES JUMPING OFF A CLIFF AND DIVING THROUGH THE AIR AS BOTH REALLY FUN, AND REALLY INTENSE!

THE WORLD'S WILDEST COASTS

There are some incredible coasteering spots around the world, where the views and the drops combine for the ultimate jumps.
For elite coasteerers, here are the best drops.

The Wild Atlantic Way

Where: Ireland

The draw: choppy, wild waters, and 50-feet (15 m) drops for miles and miles

Cape Town

Where: South Africa

The draw: a rough and rugged coast, beautiful beaches, and amazing wildlife

Kaş

Where: Turkey

The draw: beautiful views, stunning waters, and the possibility of swimming with turtles

Mallorca

Where: the Balearic Islands

The draw: turquoise waters and hidden coves and caves

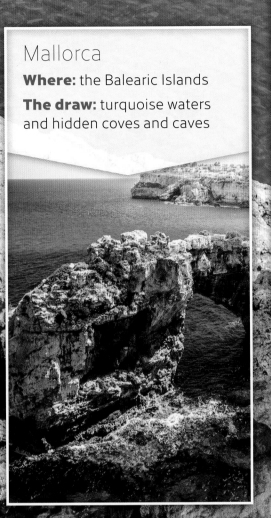

Crete

Where: the Greek Islands

The draw: sandy beaches and huge cliffs

Ngari Capes Marine Park

Where: Australia

The draw: steep cliffs and amazing sea life, including rays and sharks

Arrabida Natural Park

Where: Portugal

The draw: amazing beaches and waters

EXTREME GLOSSARY

adrenaline a hormone, or chemical messenger, in the body, that creates a sense of excitement and a surge of energy

aligned positioned to line up with something

archeologists people who study human history by analyzing things left behind by people who lived long ago

athletes people who take part in sports, often competing at a high level

buoyant able to float

captivate attract people's attention

cave network a connected system of underground caves and passages

channel a narrow area of water between two areas of land through which ships and boats often travel

chronic intense and continuing over a long period of time

crest the highest point of a wave

currents continuous, flowing movements of water

custom-made specially designed to meet certain needs

depressed feeling sad and often low in energy

disoriented confused and unable to find a sense of direction

double paddle a paddle with a blade at each end

eardrum a delicate part of the inner ear that vibrates when sound waves travel to it

elated feeling very happy

elite the best at something

endurance able to do something, such as a physical activity, for a long time

evidence information that proves something is true

exhilarating very exciting and pleasurable

expanse a wide-open area

exposure experiencing something

extreme sportspeople people who do high-risk sports

fossilized turned into a fossil, which is the hardened remains of something that lived long ago

fresh water water that does not contain salt, usually found in lakes and rivers

gravity the force that pulls objects toward other large objects

guideline a rope or line that helps guide divers through an underwater cave or network of caves

heart rates the number of times that hearts beat per minute

hormone a chemical messenger in the body that makes it do or feel certain things

inflatable able to inflate, or get bigger, when filled with air

inland farther into the land away from the coast

kayakers people who travel across water in boats called kayaks

legend a term often used to describe a person whose achievements are extremely great

lose consciousness to go into a sleep-like state and become unaware of one's surroundings

maneuver to move skillfully or carefully

modest describes someone who does not talk about their achievements or their talents

mummified preserved either by natural or human-made means; a preserved body is called a mummy

navigated traveled using a series of actions or a specified course

offshore away from the shoreline and out to sea

oxygen a gas that most living things need to survive

oxygen tanks containers filled with oxygen and used for diving below the surface of the water

Polynesian Islands a group of islands in the central and southern parts of the Pacific Ocean

powerboat a boat that has a powerful motor and can travel quickly across the surface of the water

pressures forces that act on an object

professional describes a person who does a sport or another activity as a way of earning money

propel to push forward

pursuit an aim or a goal

rigid very stiff

salt water water that contains salt, found in the oceans, seas, and some lakes

Scandinavian countries the countries in Northern Europe that include Denmark, Norway, Sweden, and Finland

schools groups of fish

stalactites hard formations that hang from the ceilings of caves. They are formed over many years when water containing minerals drips from the cave ceiling

stalagmites hard formations that rise from the floors of caves. They are formed over many years when water containing minerals drips from the cave ceiling

strait a narrow passage of water that connects two larger areas of water

streamlined designed to easily move through water or air

submerged covered by water

swimming buoy a floating device that helps swimmers stay on the water's surface

therapy a treatment to improve a person's physical or mental health

traded bought, sold, or exchanged

trading the process of buying, selling, or exchanging

tragedy a very sad event

traumatic describes something that is very upsetting

treacherous describes something that is full of danger

triathletes sportspeople who compete in triathlons, which are events that include swimming, running, and cycling

trophy an object given as a reward for an achievement

undertows strong underwater currents

visibility how well something can be seen

wetsuit a suit worn in the water to keep people warm and dry

whitewater wild and frothy water

yacht a boat used for fun or racing

FIND OUT MORE

BOOKS

DISCOVER MORE ABOUT EXTREME SPORTS WITH THESE GREAT READS.

Boone, Mary. *Surfing* (Extreme Sports). North Star Editions, 2022.

Eason, Sarah. *Dig Deep! Extreme Land Sports* (Ultimate Sports). Cheriton Children's Books, 2024.

Eason, Sarah. *Don't Look Down! Extreme Air Sports* (Ultimate Sports). Cheriton Children's Books, 2024.

Eason, Sarah. *Freeze Your Fear! Extreme Snow and Ice Sports* (Ultimate Sports). Cheriton Children's Books, 2024.

Lyon, Drew. *Surfing and Other Extreme Water Sports* (Natural Thrills). Capstone Press, 2020.

Watson, Jessica. *True Spirit: The Aussie Girl Who Took on the World*. Hachette, 2023.

WEBSITES AND ORGANIZATIONS

THESE WEBSITES ARE GREAT FOR LEARNING MORE ABOUT THE WORLD OF WATER SPORTS, AND IF YOU WANT TO TRY YOUR HAND AT SOME OF THEM, YOU CAN START YOUR JOURNEY HERE.

The American Canoe Association (ACA) has a lot of information about kayaking programs and camps for teens and young children across the United States. If you are interested in kayaking, you can learn more at this information-packed website: **www.americancanoe.org**

Learn more about sailing and available courses if you are interested in trying out this amazing sport at the American Sailing Association (ASA): **https://asa.com**

Surfline provides information on surfing schools, camps, and programs suitable for those interested in surfing across the United States and other parts of the world. Find out more at: **www.surfline.com**

Discover more about open water swimming at the USA Swimming website: **www.usaswimming.org/swimmers-parents/swimmers/open-water**

Find out more about waterskiing and wakeboarding at the USA Water Ski & Wake Sports website: **www.usawaterski.org**

Publisher's note to educators and parents:
All the websites featured above have been carefully reviewed to ensure that they are suitable for students. However, many websites change often, and we cannot guarantee that a site's future contents will continue to meet our high standards of educational value. Please be advised that students should be closely monitored whenever they access the Internet.

INDEX

ABOUT THE AUTHOR

Sarah Eason is an experienced children's book author who has written many books about sport and sport science. She would love to visit some of the amazing places researched while writing this book, and (maybe!) try out some extreme sports there.